1·05

REFLECTIONS

by

Catherine Baird

SALVATIONIST PUBLISHING AND SUPPLIES, LTD.,
JUDD STREET, KING'S CROSS, LONDON WC1H 9NN

© The Salvation Army 1975
First published 1975
ISBN 0 85412 274 5

COLONEL CATHERINE BAIRD
has been a Salvation Army officer since 1915. *She served in South Africa and the United States of America before being appointed to editorial and literary work at International Headquarters. She retired from the position of Literary Secretary in* 1957.

MADE AND PRINTED IN GREAT BRITAIN
BY THE CAMPFIELD PRESS
ST. ALBANS, HERTS.

CONTENTS

iii

FOREWORD

THE gift of insight and the mastery of expression which these poems evidence need no commendation from me. With all other readers, I can only give thanks both for them and the author, for she and her work are fruits of The Salvation Army tree which continually surprise the unknowing by their variety and delicacy.

The Colonel is my senior—for she was an officer of The Salvation Army before I had given that high calling even a moment's thought. She was the editor—and held the appointment for nineteen years—of *The Young Soldier* (a children's religious paper with a weekly circulation of a quarter of a million copies) before ever I set foot inside International Headquarters. Later, for good measure, she took over the editorship of the Army's world youth magazine as well, and ended her official active service as Literary Secretary to the General.

Yet this is the third volume of her poems to be published. Hers is the rare possession of a creative mind which could also meet the unforgiving deadlines of press days. She may look slight in body, but showed herself possessed of an inner strength which enabled her to continue to live in the top flat of a three-storied Victorian house in a south-west London suburb through the daily hazards of the blitz. She is now eighty years of age, but her mind remains alert and questioning; her heart is as outgoing as ever; and, as these pages bear witness, her spirit is still open to those divine intimations which testify to the reality of things unseen.

Those into whose hands this collection of sixty poems may come will realize to whom the ' Lines to a Writer ' could be addressed. To the author herself!

FREDERICK COUTTS,
General (R.).

Redemption

SHOW me Thyself, O perfect Love!
    My love was fashioned in the world;
It bears the marks of earth.
Art Thou above and underneath
And reaching out on either side
Beyond all measurement, all thought,
Or, art Thou as the summer morn
Whose beauty springs from stormy death
And silently relinquished life?
These are but images I see
When groping in eternity,
And, in Thy meadowlands I find,
Deep-rooted, Christ, the living Vine;
Now, humbly, willingly I come,
In Him to join my love with Thine,
Awaiting Thy redeeming power.

A search that began with earliest officership and has never ended,
nor ever will.

The New Lieutenant

SHE came from sloping plains among the hills,
    Where sun had gilded fields of corn and, in
Her youthful cheeks, still boasted of his wealth.
Now, in the sorrowing city she could hear
The thunderings of sin and see the flash
Of evil strike his victims till they lay
In hideous helplessness where'er she walked.

I

So in amaze and terror she passed by
Folding a cloak about her, lest one see
Her priestly dress and call for comfort, warmth.
Her virgin heart was cold with knowledge new
And awful. This foul place was hell! Now hate,
A wanton wind, her soul's white covering tore,
Blinded her eyes and left her naked, lost.
'Twas then she felt dry lips upon her brow,
An old and tattered garment 'round her thrown.
' Dear child,' a harlot spoke, ' I love you so!
And bless sweet innocence, and if I sneer
'Tis but to camouflage my faith in good.
Take these poor rags and hasten to your fields
Of sun-drenched peace. Your gently lowing beasts
Are worthier charge for you than I can be.
Leave me to die; fate owes me nothing else.'
Then was there silence longer than the years.
The girl, with tears, received the faded gown,
Pressed young, soft lips upon the fevered ones:
' Here I abide,' she vowed; ' you recompensed
My hate with love and clothed my nakedness
With all you owned. You're nearer God than I;
For God is love, and loveless innocence
Is like a clean, white platter without food,
To set before the hungry and the sick.'
They stood together in the darkening street,
And Love laid fingers on the girl's sad eyes,
Till she could see in those black lanes, the sun
That spread his golden mantle o'er high hills,
Reach down to clothe the harlot, sending back
His bright reflection from her weary face.

Throughout history God has used many means of revealing
Himself to man. He used the people of the ghetto of crime and
misery to show the young Lieutenant that self-righteousness is the
ugliest of all sins. Moral rectitude apart from the love of God made
known in Jesus Christ is without doubt a ' clean platter ' offered
empty to the starving.

They Wanted a Shepherd

THEY wanted a shepherd, they said,
    Dreaming of one who would
Lead them where the grass was
Bountiful, cool and green,
And the quiet waters rippled
Gently, sounding like voices speaking peace.
They were sure the new shepherd
Would satisfy them with delectable food
To save them from the
Terrors of death, leading them at
Last to indestructible mansions.

It was such a shock
When the Shepherd came never mentioning green pastures!
His eyes were filled with compassionate love—for the lost.
And His feet shod as for a rocky road.
He scanned the crowd for
Some sign of His own passion
Shining in them.

Only a few of the faithful went after the Shepherd,
Stones, instead of pastures, was their lot,
And sometimes, following the lost so dear to the Shepherd,
They plunged into the deep, dark tossing waters of sorrow,
Hearing a mocking voice crying: ' What about the still waters ? '

But the more closely they followed the Shepherd
The more certain they were that He was leading them
To a place too black and treacherous for any save God to
    penetrate.
If they wanted to be with God
They must abide with the Shepherd
Seeking the lost wherever the lost might be.
Truly they were walking in the valley of the shadow of death—
    for

Death was all around on
Every side—but God
Was smiling at death,
And when He smiled death disappeared,
Even as a mist dissolves,
Disclosing a view surpassing all finite beauty.
Fear departed, for the faithful knew now that death was neither
    evil nor fearful.
They understood the green pastures, still waters, protection,
And laden tables were the inner wealth
Of communion with the Eternal and known to
Those who follow the Good Shepherd on His perilous journey
    to seek the lost,
And on their journey are at Home
Forever in the House of the Lord.

The new Captain, they said, was not a shepherd. When they
met to drink tea together he was not there. Unkind words fell about
him like sharp stones, cutting and wounding. But the man in the
public house welcomed his cheerful, kindly voice and the ragged
old man with whom none desired to sit, leaned on his arm. Perceiving his wounds, I thought of the Good Shepherd leaving the
ninety and nine to seek the lost and of the few who went with Him
spilling their blood with His, knowing His grief and joy, walking in
eternity *now*.

A Chance to Rise Again

WHERE courage lives there also lurks defeat,
    Stalking his prey;
Or where the soldier falls bloodstained and prostrate,
Beyond the stirring sound of battle's glory-call,
There laughs Apollyon, and the hellish echo of his mirth
Pierces like scorching darts the low-bowed head
Of him who fell, facing the foe.

Faint not, thou gallant warrior,
When the black fumes of grim discouragement
Would suffocate the hope within thy breast.
Look up! See where the gathering clouds
Are pierced by burning radiance—His Cross—
The Great High Priest touched with the feeling
Of our poor infirmities.

Hark! Hear Him speak! ' O Soul, I too have known defeat;
The chilly hour when all the purpose of God's will
Appeared frustrated.
Life's toil, and agony and tears spent all in vain;
When Judas touched his unclean lips to Mine,
And Peter trembled at the mention of My name
As though 'twere charged with plague,
E'en John, friend of My bosom, slept
While I carried a world's gross load of sin,
In lone Gethsemane. I know defeat.

The dumb, whose lips responded to My touch,
Raised not his voice in My behalf:
The lame man stood afar nor followed Me
Up the steep slopes of Calvary.
And he whose eyes first saw the light in Me,
Stood with the multitude gazing in vulgar curiosity
While I was lifted up—and bled—and died.
O Soul, I too have known defeat.

They laid My wounded body in a tomb,
Sealed it, the while a mad world cried:
' Death has defeated righteousness, alas! '
And others, devil-driven, gleefully proclaimed
The triumphing of wrong.

They thought the things men did to Me
Could stay the strength of God whose silent power
Can overthrow the noisome efforts
Of earth's mightiest princes.

Drugged by the opiate of ignorance,
The sceptic wrote upon my grave:
' This is the end.' 'Twas not. *I rose again!*

That Cross, gleaming amid the dark, lifted Me high
Above the grasp of sin and death;
That Cross means victory, and not defeat.
Defeat is but a phantom thing—a stone
Sealing the tomb;
Fling it aside! Then thou shalt rise again.

O baffled, disappointed one,
The Voice that wakened sleeping souls and dead,
Bids thee arise! Come forth! Challenge thy foes!
The wounds men gave to thee, God glorifies;
Through them, thrice healed, thou shalt confound the strong.

Soldier—where courage lives, there also lurks defeat,
Where'er defeat, a chance to rise again!

    I was very young when this was written. ' Should you put words into the mouth of Jesus ? ' I was asked. Is it not a certainty that Jesus, when nearing death, *felt* forsaken ? Thus His voice reaches us across the centuries, speaks in every experience, trial or joy. The two greatest saints I was privileged to know, when nearing death experienced a period of darkness. What had taken a lifetime to build seemed to crumble and fall upon the wearied spirit. But they heard the voice of One they had served untiringly reminding them of Life that death cannot kill. For us Jesus died, yet by a divine paradox, He has never died.

Whom Having Not Seen Ye Love

THE Holy Land lies 'neath an Eastern sun
    That warmed her breast through years when Jesus spoke
Deep wisdom, new and strange, yet old as God.
O blessed countryside where, clothed in flesh,
The Son of God preached grace and truth and light!
Blue Galilee, your white-capped waves beat soft
Upon the silver sands where Jesus stood;
Methinks I hear you chanting o'er again
The living words He uttered by your shores:
' I am the Bread of Life, and he who comes
To Me shall never hunger, never thirst.'

The winds come singing from the hills and plains,
Echoing loud His deep reverberate voice:
'A new commandment give I unto you:
Love ye each other as I have loved you.'

Time and the elements have washed away
His footprints from the sands of Galilee,
Still I can see them luminous and clear,
Where every budding blade and open flower
Repeats the Master's call, ' Rise, follow Me! '

I never saw the splendour of His face
When, in the storm, He ordered ' Peace, be still! '
I never heard the music of His voice
Fluting glad tidings of eternal hope;
I never knelt beside His flowing robes,
Nor bathed His feet with my repentant tears,
Nor stood I with the multitude who ate
Of that abundant feast beside the sea;
Yet I am blessed with those who saw the Christ,
For He who walked on earth now lives in me,
And I am numbered with the honoured men
Who, having never seen, truly believe!

In Tune

GOD sings His lyric songs among the trees,
    His feet tread lightsome, where the hurrying breeze
Blows cool across the golden-daisied fields,
Or where the warm brown earth her fruitage yields.
I wander through His cornfields and His lanes,
Seeing through finite, ofttimes wistful eyes,
The hills, the dim-lit valleys and the plains,
Like grand orchestral music harmonize.
Enchanted soul I silently commune
With Him: ' Harmonious God, my heart attune!
In all this grand accord I would not be
The lonely harp whose notes discord with Thee.'

God's Reckless Son

IF I have fellowship with Him
    I shall pursue
A way untrodden by the multitudes
    And loved by few!

My lot shall be to speak a word
    That, seeming new,
Makes me a stranger in the house of friends—
    As He was, too!

I would adventure recklessly,
    O reckless Son,
Who staked Thy life against the world,
    And lost—and *won*!

Every crisis demands some sort of choice, and in making a choice, not through an isolated text, but in the light of the entire spirit prevailing in the life of Jesus Christ, we often discover what for us

8

is a new aspect of truth. These lines were written shortly before the Second World War when I could find no reconciliation between the example of Jesus and the iniquities of war. I came to see that the end of world-scale strife must begin through the individual being at peace with God, ending inner conflict and bitterness toward any man. The ideal might never be achieved in this material world, but if we labour for it here and now whatever the cost, we can leave the finished work to God.

One Startled Moment

(O)NE startled moment came the heavens near,
  So near, so aweful that I ceased to hear,
Inhale, or taste, or feel, or even see
Aught time had promised for delight or dread.
This was the moment of my need and fear,
Of waking from a child's confusing dream,
A lonely moment; then the heavens came near.
Now are the years no longer years to me,
I lose them all in one great, glowing beam:
The moment that is my eternity,
A perfect instant, bright with God, complete,
To test my days and hours in furnace heat
Till all that cannot live in fire be dead.

Have you, too, known popularity? Is it not like a fog hindering us from standing face to face with ourselves seeing a little of what God must see. The day when all men approve our actions is more testing than the hour when, in spite of opposition and even of false witness, we are enabled by God's grace to stand by what we believe to be true. In such an hour of distress, God came. This was the 'startled moment' when the eternal life became real and very present.

The Gift

FATHER, I bring my sorrow unto Thee;
  Too small I am to hold it, and too weak
To bear it fruitfully along the years;
Too complex is this grief for understanding
  By human candle-light.
I scan each particle and mark, with shock,
My shameful fear of watching suffering face to face.
Blended with loss I find the agony of knowing
My best is scarcely better than my worst:
I pray Thee wash self-pity from my heart
While staggering toward Thine open arms
With my new offering, my costly gift;
Oh, yes, I know it is a gift—the largest I shall e'er receive.
Show me, for I am still a child,
How I may use a treasure, bright with tears,
As buried seed that glorifies the dust
And spreads abundance where the hungry wait.

Written after watching suffering and death. Once we realize that sorrow, though not a gift from God, is an experience we can offer to Him, He will purify our emotions, causing darkness with Him to be brighter than light without Him.

The Healer Lives
'And great multitudes followed Him, and He healed them all'
(Matthew 12: 15).

WHEN daylight waned,
  The desolate drew near to Him;
Their sighing stirred
The twilight's tranquil hush.
Wistful, in weakness,
Faltering in faith, but still
They came to Jesus—and
He healed them all!

They come today:
Their caravan, unending,
From everywhere,
Winds its bewildered way;
O where is He
Once sought in old Jerusalem?
I hear it whispered,
He was crucified!

If He be dead,
Then every smile forever fades!
If He be gone,
Each bruisèd reed must break!
And if He cometh not,
The world, confounded,
Must meet—each man—at last
His certain fate.

But, fret thou not,
For needless is thy troubling;
The Healer lives!
His hurrying footsteps run
Where'er His friends,
Moved by the Christ within them
Pass through the portals
Of earth's ruined homes.

Through them, He bows;
I see Him gently cleansing
A leper's wound.
Or, watching through the night,
Cool lies His hand
Upon a weary sufferer,
Till calmness settles
On the fevered night!

He's walking now
Through sad, war-ridden by-ways,
His eye is grave,
But gentle is the arm
That raises up the wounded little children,
And folds love's mantle
Round the poor, bereaved!

The Healer lives!
Then needless is thy troubling,
His hurrying footsteps
Race against the night,
For ere the daylight wanes
The blind shall see Him
Stoop as He did of old
To heal them all!

Written for *All the World* with the growing realization that so long as dedicated men and women work for the good of their fellows Christ can be seen walking in this troubled world. ' Could ye not watch with Me one brief hour? ' He asked His disciples in the hour of His agony. It is cheering to consider the long, lone vigil of those who tend the sick, stoop to tend the leper or seek to bring about the reconciliation of unfriendly peoples. These often unknown saints, however humble, watch with Him.

A Child No More

(O) WE would worship Jesus
　　　When He lay in Mary's arms,
A helpless Babe bound by His infancy!
Word of the living God, but speechless,
Stronger than death and hell,
Yet in humanity confined:
Our hearts are drawn to weakness;
What of might?

Are we afraid, dismayed
Because the Holy Child, a Child no more,
Breaks through the swaddling bands
Of man's embrace
And makes the captor captive?
Or do our ears delight to hear Him speak
Truth that astonishes the mind
Awakening the spirit's cry?

O may we join the worshippers
Who pass with Jesus from His infancy,
Nor seek to cradle Him in timid thought,
Or stay His feet from peril's lonely path,
Choosing to watch Him grow!
May we, with them,
Forever finding God in Christ,
Receive the Bread and Wine
That quickens intellect and will,
Bestowing power to support a cross
And praise the Victor who had led us there.

Are we not sometimes content to remain adoring the Babe of Bethlehem? Is it not easy so to do? But this Child grew and became strong. At first His little shoulders could bear no greater burden than going home and being subject to His parents. But because He was obedient in immediate matters He was strong enough to bear the burden of our world's redemption. We may not linger in the stable.

Ask, Seek, Knock

HE bids thee ask; then do not fear
        Thy spirit's questionings;
The mind that asketh not must surely be
Dark as a dungeon, locked and windowless.
As the first stirring of thy soul His answer comes
And light, as much as thou canst bear,
        Spreadeth about thee.

13

He bids thee seek; leaving the prison of no faith;
E'en though, with human fault, thou seekest life
In barren places where no flowers thrive,
He will abide with thee
As, mid the shades and shame of earth,
Thou findest Him, the Lamp of God,
Treading the highway where the verdant slopes
Are bright with blossoms dancing in the sun.

He bids thee knock; then He who died
To guide thy footsteps Home
Walketh before thee
When, at the highest level of thy sacred quest,
The soul's insistent wings beat on the Father's heart,
The doors swing open and thy spirit, free,
Enters, in Jesus' name, to share a life with God.

The Call of God

JESUS calls from field and city
  Through confused and fearful cries
From bewildered, stricken masses
  Or a widow's stifled sighs;
    Louder than the war-drum's sound,
    Soft as tears that stain the ground.

Jesus calls where'er the suffering
  Bear their anguish all alone,
Homeless, loveless, lost and fainting,
  Needing bread, yet offered stone;
    Calls for intellect and will,
    Calls for dedicated skill.

Jesus' call comes closer, closer,
From the weary, desolate,
From the friend who stands beside us
Or the stranger at the gate;
Can I fold within my care
Truth He bids me now to share?

Jesus calls. His Cross assures me
Of redemption's deepest spring:
Love transforming, multiplying
Whatsoever gifts I bring;
I would in that love abide,
Serving men at Jesus' side.

Jesus, Word of God, I hear Thee
Calling from amid the throng;
I am coming in my weakness,
Fearing not for Thou art strong;
All things I can do through Thee;
Live Thy life and love through me.

As a girl I visited my sister and her husband stationed in charge
of the Pretoria Corps in South Africa. I was impressed by a scroll
hanging on the hall wall offering aid to any in need, and signed:
'Servants of all for Christ's sake.' Throughout their lives these
servants fulfilled their promise. As time passed I saw that the desire
to serve is God's call. Thus, in order to use God-given talents, we
are constrained to develop them through industry and study, the
extent of our efforts being the measure of our desire to serve. All
are called to serve humanity. Some may be moved by the sight of
poverty and hunger or disease and sin; others by a deep sense of
responsibility for interpreting the word of God through preaching
or teaching, never forgetting that all Christly service, even the giving
of a cup of cold water, teaches and preaches that word.

His Voice

BEAUTIFUL the call of Jesus
  Clear and strong in Galilee,
Calling to the heights of service
  Men who harvested the sea;
Gladly they obeyed His summons,
  Followed wheresoe'er He trod,
Till with sight transformed by loving
  They beheld the face of God.

Jesus called them to communion,
  Led them to His Father's heart,
Named them friends and gave them courage
  For their burden-sharing part;
Sent them forth to carry tidings
  Of a new and living way
Where the night, with Him, is brighter
  Than the glory of the day.

When the call of Jesus sounded
  From the peak of Calvary,
Clouds of fear and bitter anguish
  Veiled the glorious mystery;
But the faithful meekly waited,
  Bound together by His call,
And when morning dawned they hailed Him
  Risen Saviour, Lord of all.

Ye who know the call of Jesus,
  Come rejoicing, listening still
To His measureless unfolding
  Of our Heavenly Father's will;
Blessed are the friends of Jesus,
  Poverty is wealth with Him,
And the way of life eternal
  Is the love no power can dim.

Contemplation

MY Father, when I contemplate
  The mystery of Love divine,
My heart receives a little Child,
  I kneel before His lowly shrine;
He came Thy beauty to disclose
  In this familiar earthly place,
To tell me in my native tongue
  How I may meet Thee face to face.

My Father, when I meditate
  The servant King, His heavy load,
I fain would wear a workman's dress,
  My feet shod for a rugged road;
I pray for power to be with Him
  Who, fearless, plumbed the depths of hell,
Then, for His sake, my all to give,
  His name to praise, His truth to tell.

My Father, when with awe, I view
  The fearful heights of Calvary,
I see a throne formed as a Cross,
  A glory veiled in agony;
My weakness is my offering now,
  My grief that I should ever be
Exalted save through loving Him,
  Who chose this Cross through loving me.

My Father, when my eyes behold
  The risen Lord confronting me,
I touch with confidence and faith
  The incorruptible, the free;
Here is the life that cancels death,
  O'erflowing as my vows I take,
Till from my inmost soul I say:
  All, all I do is for Thy sake.

Bread of Life

SPIRIT of God, Thou art the Bread of Heaven
    Come for my need in Jesus Christ the Lord,
Broken in Him whose life was freely given
    In deathless love He only could afford.

Thou art the Bread that satisfies forever,
    The inward health that overcomes disease,
The Love that lives through death, subsiding never,
    My secret fortress and my soul's release.

O Bread from God, I choose Thee now with gladness,
    Though sweet the taste of earthly gain may be!
My spirit pines in poverty and sadness
    Unless my sustenance be found in Thee.

Lord God, I come, Thy life in mine is waking;
    Whate'er I am I bring into Thy care;
Thy loving hands will bless me in the breaking
    Of Bread Thou gavest, and I long to share.

Journeying Safely

*' If we are really living for the Kingdom at our own expense, that
is sacrifice '* (Father Andrew).

HIS donkey had a coat of grey, shaggy and plain,
    Yet soft as plush to tired limbs;
Her patient eyes were brown as earth, and bright as new-formed
    pools of rain.
Meekly she bore her master's weight o'er rugged hills and
    treacherous roads,
Easing his journey with her strength, sparing his feet the heated
    stones.
Perhaps she sensed the gratitude in gentle hands that guided
    her,

Perhaps she halted, knowing how her master would not turn
   aside
Nor leave the wounded traveller bleeding and broken in the
   way.
Silent she waited in the sun, bending her head, and listening
For sounds remote from human ears.
Silent, with muscles swiftly braced, she watched her master's
   offering:
He used his skills to bind and heal; he spared his wealth to
   purchase care;
Most lovely gift of all, he gave his donkey's broad and supple
   back,
Lifting the drooping traveller there.
And for himself, the sharpened stones, the rising dust, the
   heavy load,
The abysmal weariness unknown to any save the ones who toil
That he who cannot walk may ride to shelter and, with strength
   restored,
May safely journey to his home.

Reflections

He scanned the hills through loving eyes:
The flowering cherry tree,
The hyacinth and daffodil,
The stream that met the sea;
The earth was a belovèd friend
From whom he soon must part,
While singing thrushes paused to take
The slow beat of his heart.

He saw an infinite design
In every beauteous thing:
The rich brown soil, the smiling rose,
A sparrow's patterned wing.
A friendly word, a kindly deed,
Like spring leaves, tender, green,
Were signals from a Quickening Source
All-powerful, though unseen.

Red poppies, velvet in the shade
Of white clouds sailing by,
Reflected, for his sight, a Realm
Where flowers never die
And gentle souls, their winters o'er,
Their silent victories won,
Shall blossom as unfolding buds
Awakened by the sun.

Describing my brother, whose life in the testimony of his friends
was a purifying agent wherever he went. He literally surrendered
all material assets in order to do what he believed to be right. Extra
sensitive to all lovely things, he used to say: ' I need not possess
what I see. If I love and appreciate beauty it is mine.' He would
have joined Plato saying: 'As artificial light is to the sun, so is the
sun itself to ultimate reality.'

20

Calling More Fools

' *We are fools for Christ's sake* ' (1 Corinthians 4: 10, R.S.V.).

PASSING beyond the worldly wise
    He toiled, with bright unguarded eyes,
Seeking to bring the lost
Homeward at any cost.
We gave our gold his poor to feed,
We smiled on every selfless deed,
We cheered, applauding, when he bled;
' He is a noble fool! ' we said.
    Clutching our gilded crowns,
    Holding our dear renowns.

Sheltered, we sorrowed when he fell
Outside our cosy citadel,
Offering more gold, more bread
In memory of the dead.
But where his life-blood stains the sod
Sore wounded works his Shepherd God,
Calling more fools to seek the lost,
Fools who will pay the highest cost,
    For only blood avails,
    Only the Blood prevails!

The Blood is the Life, and only our offered lives can join us to Him who was Saviour of the world.

Caress of Sorrow

JOY wrapped her in a rainbow cloak
  And kissed her crimson lips; they shed
A fragrance every time she spoke;
The needy marked her raiment rare,
Her glowing eyes, untroubled smile,
Yet she had nothing they could share.
Among the wealthy she must live
For she was poor and could not give.

Sorrow o'ertook her and a thorn
Was pressed as by some ruthless hand
Where she had once sweet laurels worn;
Cold fingers lined her cheek and brow,
Dressing her dark, soft hair with frost;
The hand of grief had blessed her now.
Among the hungering poor she lives;
She is so rich she gives and gives.

Beside the Mercy Seat

HE had a troubled face
  And sometimes bitter words would slip
Too easily from tongue and lip,
Darting like sudden sparks from ugly fires
Of deep resentment and of proud desires.

  I thought—judging his words—
  His goal was just as high as earth
  And that his measuring of worth
Was taken always by a badge of rank,
Of treasure weighed and counted in the bank.

22

But once I saw him new,
Silent, as though an angel hand
Had touched his lips. I saw him stand
As one communing in the courts above,
His meek eyes quiet, purified by love.

Which man is he? I ask.
The discontented one of yesterday?
Or this, with striving washed away,
Surveying now, with happiness complete,
A sinner kneeling at the Mercy Seat?

Are there two men? Or one
Who made a covenant with God
Long since, and faltered where he trod?
And has he loosed his hold on worldly dross,
Moved by this sinner praying at the Cross?

The servant named by God
For holy skills and loving art
May not from his true name depart;
To be another he cannot afford
For near the sinner he is near his Lord.

A King in the Band

JOHN plays a trombone in our Army band
    Each Sunday: but through every week
He labours on the land his father left
When John was but a laughing, carefree lad,
Seeing bright visions of life's unscaled heights
Beckoning his aspiring soul to climb
Where victory stands, with laurels in her hand,
Ready to pass them to the venturesome.

Though suns of youth still sparkle in his eyes,
His strong, broad shoulders droop, and in his hair
The silver gleams like rivers in the dark.
Mind of a poet—John writes out his lines
In daily toil, his fine hand on a plough.
On wintry days he wears a threadbare coat;
Yet in John's cot a brother's orphaned babes,
Rounded of limb and fair to look upon,
All warmly clad, play in the firelight
Upon the hearth—and on his tender care
A widowed mother leans with confidence.

I once saw John upon the snow-touched hills
(I and my sister, on our way to town),
A wounded lamb lay quiet in his arms
As John trudged upward to his hillside home.
' Ho, John! ' I cried, ' Come with us to the hall! '
But, pointing to the lamb, John shook his head,
Flashed us a smile, and strode on up the hill.
I looked at Mary, Mary looked at me . . .
Flushed, paled, and flushed again. Her lovely eyes
Pleaded, ' Don't make his burden heavier still.'
We did not speak—just watched John climbing on,
A wounded lamb contented in his arms—
But, as we turned upon our way, I knew
Quite suddenly, how great a man was John!

Through cheerless years, John whistles on his way,
He comes, he goes, at morn, at noon, at night.
The neighbours see a shabby, common man
Toiling along a narrow hillside path—
I see a prince upon a shining steed
Ride forth, unarmed, alone to meet the foe.

Yet in the morn no herald sings a song
Of love's bright conquest and the end of self.
At eventide a labourer, they say,

Dusty and tired, turns in a cottage gate;
Strange, I see no one save the king
Pass through the portals of his castle home.

If rank be written on the heart, and men
Are crowned for noble deeds, not royal blood,
When Jesus comes I think He'll give a throne
To John who plays the trombone in our band,
Or to some kindly shepherd of the fields,
Or little serving maid—or maybe, you!

At first I saw John only on Sundays playing the trombone.
Though I appreciated his talent, I never really knew him until,
visiting his mother, I discovered in John more than a musician. He
represents a multitude of bandsmen all over the Army world whose
work behind the scenes is an act of worship even greater than their
most perfect musical performance.

One Word for Judas

JUDAS! The name is stained with treason,
    Bleakest tragedy and ignominious death;
He, for a handful of bright coins,
Betrayed the Holy One of God.

This treachery did Judas seal with the
Salute of brotherhood—a kiss,
And, at the sign, soldiers fell upon Christ
With swords and cudgels
As though He were a bandit.

Now Jesus knew that He must die,
And, with this knowledge,
Had a high wisdom born of fellowship
With God that gave Him power

To look at death serenely.
Had He not told His followers:
' Do not fear those who kill the body
But cannot kill the soul ' ?

Judas had listened then,
Thrilling to feast upon the words of life.

How terrible to realize their truth
On a dark night that throbbed with hate and fear,
While sword-blades split the gloom
Like lightning flashes,
And every friendly face vanished from the scene
As falling stars pass quietly from sight!

But Jesus, though He seemed to walk with soldiers,
Walked with God. And He was calm.

Not so with Judas the fugitive from grace,
Knowing that, while his Master prayed,
He had made contract with the devil.
When Jesus was condemned, sin's consequence,
Like loosened rocks upon a mountainside,
Overtook Judas.
Soon they would pin him, crushed to earth.
Could he perchance undo the wrong?
But no! The priests stared with contempt
As Judas flung the filthy silver at their feet,
And ran, demented, bruised, battered, harassed,
To a place beyond all reason
Where he hanged himself.

Yet once his name was honoured in Judea,
For warriors had enhanced it, made it fair;
So, when a boy was born in Kerioth,
His happy parents named him Judas.
His mother, smiling at her son,
May well have longed that he might be

A man with honest eyes
Searching for Israel's true Deliverer,
Strong in His defence.

No one can tell when Judas made his first
Surrender to himself.
But at some point along the way with Christ,
The light of loyalty had weakened, waned.
Thus, when he came to his immortal hour,
The fragile flame went out.

One word for Judas:
He took all the blame for vileness;
Said no word of cruel priests,
Frightened disciples or the faltering procurator.
' I have betrayed innocent blood! ' he cried, ' I,'
In anguished tones for all the world to hear
Through all the ages;
And he did not point at me!

I sometimes try to follow Judas where he went
Into the yawning chasms of despair;
But his are paths too dangerous for me,
Too dark and terrifying.
Only the Lord of Light dare tread
The treacherous realms where demons rave;
His love alone can reach the unutterable void
And seek out Judas,
Calling to him again in those last awful moments
Of repentant grief.

Good Friday

(O)NLY Jesus, one with God,
    Felt bereavement's fiercest tearing,
Trod the measureless abyss
Named in the word ' forsaken ';
Who could know hell's desolation ?
    Only Jesus, one with God!

Home to Thee

I WOULD go silently,
    Lord, when I come to Thee;

Glide as some gallant barque
Into the mighty dark.

Softly and gently ride
O'er the receding tide;

Steer from the shores of time
T'ward an eternal clime.

Lord, on a quiet sea
Let me sail home to Thee.

The Servant

T HIS is how God's servant pays
    For the gift of His employ:
Bleeding hands and wounded feet
Empty purse and harrowed heart!

Is there no reward at all
For the lowly serving man?
Yes! He hears the angels sing,
Sees the shining, guiding star,
Follows till he finds the Son
Greatest servant ever born;
Now he throws his purse away
Now his hands are stronger far,
Now his feet more swiftly run,
And he has a larger heart,
Broader shoulders shaped to share
Jesus' world-redeeming power.

Written because so many worthy people still expect righteousness
to be rewarded with this world's benefits.

Lost in Christ

IF Jesus calls, ' Launch out into the deep! '
    Turn thy ship boldly toward the open sea,
Nor hug the coastline of familiar thought,
However dark mysterious distance seems.
When those, preferring safety and untruth,
Mock thy departing from their cherished shore,
Naming thee traitor, alien, have no care:
The winds are God's and, should thy vessel break
Plunging thee where the deepest waters are,
Be not affrighted: thou art lost in Christ,
And all who search for thee shall find thy God.

To Sleep

(O)UR Robin sits with father, Sunday morns,
　　His fair head high, his short legs swinging out
The tempo of the sacred songs we sing;
'Tis five whole joyous years since he was born,
And Robin thinks he surely is a man.
So—when the music halts, and Captain speaks
About the Israelites and their long march
Through wilderness and seas and plains and hills,
Though Robin's head begins to nod a bit—
I dare not offer him my empty lap!

The sermon lengthens and, at long, long last,
He really cannot shoo away the sleep
That teases him, and with a heaviness
Tugs at his eyelids and brings down his chin
To rest upon his muffler, while he sways—
He sways—and he would fall, but father's arm
Enfolds and holds him close, and he is safe,
And I am calm again, but pondering,
For now I seem to see another child,
Twice Robin's height, and yet, to God—a child.

He feels full competent to face the whole
Of life.　He scorns to lean upon
The pity or the strength of any man.
He has a work to do; what cares he then
If zeal consume him in the pressing hours
Or, if his body die?　Upon its ruin
Perchance some soul shall step toward the sky.
His cares grow large, storms rage; still he endures.
A long, deep sleep o'erwhelms him and he sways.
He sways, but does not fall, for God is there,

Reaching His long, kind, everlasting arm
To rest beneath the eager spirit till
Once more he wakes, refreshed, to live anew.

Based on the belief that nothing, not even death, can separate
us from the love of God which is in Christ Jesus.

Two Questions

IF a fool should seek
    To hold the wind
In his sinewy fingers,
    Could he bind
The breeze that breathes
    O'er piquant pine
And finding her fragrance,
    Makes it mine?

Can the hurtful hand
    Of this day of care
Capture or crush
    A lifelong prayer
That woos and wins eternity
    And folds her
        Timelessness in me?

Thou Art the Life

AND could I boast?
    I am the plant. Thou art the Life
That surges in all tender waiting things,
Wrestling with death in winter,
But in spring
Spreading the blush of health in leaf and stem.
    God, if some beauty steals through me, 'Tis Thine.
How could I boast?

How easy it is to think our good deeds are our own. Nothing beautiful or true comes from any other than God. The humanist might do well to acknowledge this fact.

The Christ Child

IN every youthful face I see
    The Christ Child smiling down on me;
For once, upon a night of joy,
And clothèd in a little Boy,
God, in sweet majesty came near;
His voice was young and passing clear,
Awakening the heart in me
And calling: ' I have need of thee! '

Good News
' *Come ye yourselves apart . . . and rest a while* ' (Mark 6: 31).

COME into the open; toss the latest paper down;
    O never mind the placards that are stirring up our town,
    For here is news—*good news!*
'Tis not about the atom pile, the riots or the pound,
Nor where, in case of flood or flame, a shelter may be found;
    My news—*good news!*

This morning very early, without the slightest sound,
A blade of grass pressed upward from her hiding underground;
A rosebud shyly opened up a secret treasure chest,
And, shaking out a velvet gown, how silently she dressed!
The warm winds bore her fragrance o'er the meadows by the
    sea,
And, passing by my window, poured it freely over me.
    My news—*good news!*

O listen to the heart-beats of the sunny summerlands!
A lad has left his horses while beside the sea he stands,
His hands are rough with toiling; his head, as ever, bare,
The friendly winds come frolicking to rumple up his hair;
An ordinary fellow, knowing kinship with the sod,
Yet, this morning, very early, his soul communed with God.
    My news—*good news!*

Although the newspapers forecast war, I found it incredible that
mankind had learned nothing from the glaring truth that wars
aggravate rather than solve international problems. Yet, coming
from my ' digs ' one morning *en route* for 101 Queen Victoria Street,
I encountered busy workmen digging underground shelters. Outside
my office overlooking the Thames, newspaper boys were shouting
ominous messages from the headlines. Evidently men had learned
nothing. Just before the blitzkrieg began in earnest I visited friends
in Norfolk. I found it inspiring to leave the little house where the
radio blared out the woeful tidings, seeking the quiet of the open
fields and finding sustenance for the tragic experiences that lay
ahead. The Salvationist, of course, cannot remain among the good
news; but he must never forget it.

Dreaming

LORD JESUS, when You were a boy, like me,
  Did You run out at evening just to see
The green-tipped meadows all aglow with light?
And listen for the sinking sun's good night?
O did You watch the barley bowing where
The breeze had breathed and left a ripple there?
And did Your heart beat loudly? Did it seem
You soared away upon a wingèd dream?

And sometimes, tell me, Jesus whom I love,
When winds came swiftly sweeping from above,
Did God seem close—and whispering to You
Gay, splendid secrets that You knew were true?
Secrets so wonderful that You could not share,
And yet so lovely You were glad to bear
A cross—because of all God said would be,
Lord Jesus, when You were a boy like me?

Across the Street

'PLEASE Miss,' she said (her voice was sweet),
  'Do take my hand across the street.'
And I, from lofty five foot four,
Looked down. She was but five, not more—
A cap of blue, a coat all torn,
Two little shoes, both scuffed and worn,
A dirty smudge upon her nose,
Brown eyes—they were not meant for prose!

I took her clinging hand in mine,
'Twas raining, yet I saw stars shine
As, glad, I led those baby feet
Across the busy, crowded street,
And while I watched her smallness race
Away, my thoughts began to chase
The brown eyes and the wee smudged nose,
Till from my soul a prayer arose:

Lord, in Thy mercy and good grace,
If we've grown tall, and if our pace
Is sure and strong, as through our days
We, fearless, move through life's strange maze,
Grant us to heed the plaintive tone
Of little ones, who've not yet grown
In wisdom. Let us guide their feet,
As through a busy, crowded street.

Nor pride ourselves, because we know
The truth it pleaseth Thee to show
To us Thy children in the street,
For once we moved with faltering feet.
So, woe to us, if ill betide
Them while they're walking by our side,
Or if we lead their steps astray
Instead of by the Living Way.

Summons to Bethlehem

STILL I am waiting near this lowly stall,
     The young lamb's bleating and the white dove's call
Mock my abiding through the centuries,
And cry out shame on my unbended knees.

35

I saw the shepherds bowing o'er Thy bed,
I watched the wise men come with reverent tread;
They journeyed far to reach this holy place,
But I was born in presence of Thy face.
O Prince of Peace, I wait, I wait, I wait;
Youth of Every Age, I hesitate.

I am not with the praising crowds who sing
And dream of triumph as they hail Thee King;
I know Thy infant crying, feeble, brief,
Preludes a rending and relentless grief;
The light that circles widely in this shed,
Is narrowing to a thorn-crown for Thy head;
Within Thy smile a welcoming God is near,
But I am unresponsive, cold with fear.

How shall I join the choir who Thee adore,
When all the songs I know are songs of war?
May I be drawn Thy garments to caress,
Clothed in this stained and dreary battledress?
And shall my sorrow be Thy summons clear
Urgently sounding on the listening ear
Of one who, at Thy word, will run to me
And, in his caring, find he worships Thee?

O wake a heaven-born band to answer ' Yes! '
A youthful band whose deeds Thy love confess,
Whose faithfulness and truth Thy might declare
Till I am startled into willing prayer.

The Christmas season with its message of peace on earth was
near; yet strife continued. Even those who firmly believed in the
Resurrection, appeared to believe that the only way to extinguish
evil was to destroy the body of him who practised it. The young
man in these lines is not a soldier. He is merely representative of
those who have been brought up in the Christian faith, but have
had no intellectual awakening, no personal confrontation with the
living Christ. But for him there is hope in that he recognizes the

stagnant uselessness of his condition, longing for youths like himself so to demonstrate the Christly life that he will go with them as Thomas, unbelieving, went with his friends to see the Risen Lord and be willing to reach out and touch those aweful wounds, thus entering into a genuine experience of God receiving the touch of a love that is the only certain way of overcoming evil.

For All who Witness

' I have prayed for thee, that thy faith fail not ' (Luke 22: 32).

I PRAY for thee—
    And not for thy release from furnace flames;
O may thy faith enduring, never fail
To see who walks beside thee in the fire,
How clear His features are in flares of pain!

    I pray for thee—
And not for Thy reward for holy aims;
O may thy faith through lonely trial prevail
And crown thee while the scorching tongues leap higher,
In Christ thy suffering, and in Christ thy reign,
    I pray for thee.

Reach the Sky

WHAT profit should we win the race
    To solve the mysteries of space,
And send new suns and satellites
To signal through ten thousand nights,
If we neglect to read the star
Shining for ever from afar
Of Jesus, cradled from His birth,
On the dark bosom of the earth?
And what are victories of skill
Unless, exploring in God's will,
We prove the law we there have found
In this our world—our holy ground?
For God is *now* and God is *here*,
Not hidden in some shadowy sphere.
Who stoops to heed another's cry
Shall touch His hand and reach the sky.

One word for All

WHEN God the Father spoke on Christmas Day,
    No eager crowds assembled, none could say
His voice came thundering on the ear
With eloquence that kindled joy or fear;
Yet, when He spoke, the chattering around
Was silenced by one simple, perfect sound:
  An infinitely penetrating call:
  One word, God's only word for all,
  New, with vast glories from above,
  This word was, is and ever shall be, *love*.

Chosen Friends

HE came as silent as the power
     That calls the daffodil in spring;
The while a world's confusèd throng
Noisily clamoured, then as now,
God walked in Christ among the dead,
Loving them into life in Him.
And some there were who followed Him
Joying to shed their blood with His
For the high prize of saving some:
The sad, the hungering and lost.
    On these He laid His load of love,
    And crownèd them His chosen friends!

Star of Hope

THERE is a Star whose all-embracing light
     Most clearly shines amid the deepening night;
A Star whose beam with unrelenting power
Leads us, unharmed, through trial's fiery hour
And signals peace when everywhere is war,
Promise of life where sin shall be no more,
Sign of a city builded by the Lord,
Founded on truth unconquered by the sword,
Home of the seeking mind, the loving heart,
From whence all fears and phantasies depart.
    Follow the Star! God's will has won
    And our lost world's redemption has begun!

New-Born Every Day

NOTHING new under the sun, they say,
    Yet Jesus is new-born every day!
Ye who receive Him, march along
To a new song, clear song. O be strong
In the Word that redeems each passing hour,
Fresher than earth's best new-born flower,
Sweeter than waters rushing down
From the mountain spring to the dusty town;
Mighty to silence our earthly strife,
Healing our wounds and restoring life;
Yes, Jesus is new-born every day!

The Seers

ONLY the lowly and the wise
    Hear victory songs in infant cries!
Proud eyes may swiftly turn away
From Jesus' manger bed of hay,
Yet do the pure, with perfect sight,
See chariots of holy light
And heavenly horsemen, clad in power
Invading time each day and hour.
In silent prayer they venture far
Beyond this world's most distant star,
Encounter God in every place
Where saint and sinner need His grace.

O Little One

(O) LITTLE ONE, how weak Thou art
    In Mary's undefended arms,
Nor horse, nor chariot, nor sword
To guard Thy life through earth's alarms!
And yet how passing strong Thou art,
How stern must Thy endurance prove
To carry in Thy infant heart
The burden of eternal love!

A Prayer for Added Wisdom

H̲E cares most earnestly about donations;
    He has a gift, quite rare, for conversations
That stir the hardened millionaire
And lead him eagerly to spare
    For worthy causes.
However weary, he will pay attention
To wary donors and, without contention,
    He'll travel, uncomplaining, to world's end,
    To claim whatever wealthy ones will spend.

Wise man! He knows that gold is good,
Since money is the price of food.
    But there his wisdom ends.

I pray, how fervently I make petition,
That to his gift be made a pure addition:
    An open mind, a kind, attentive ear
    For friend and foe who at his gate appear
      With high intention.
May he not pass them by, unheeding
The treasure of life; too swiftly speeding
    To gather what a willing, generous heart
    Would freely spill, not holding back one part.

41

O God, who knows when wounded sparrows fall,
Grant Thy divine perception to us all,
That we may see with Christly, loving eyes,
The pearl of pearls: a life, a living prize.
    Then wisdom shall begin.

An ordinary soldier's grave in France is marked 'known to God'. We do not know his name or what gifts were buried with him after man's stupidity had done its worst.

Have we not seen a friend wounded unnecessarily through lack of understanding by another? Does it not shock us into self-examination? How many times have we failed to value the character and capability of another?

An old teacher once asked the meaning of the text: 'He that calleth his brother a fool is in danger of hell fire.' The master replied: 'For me it means that any man who causes a fellow being to feel less than he is, deserves the burning remorse he must ultimately endure.'

Reverence for personality is essential to Christianity.

Lines to a Writer
'Write the things which thou hast seen' (Revelation 1: 19).

WHEN strong men lie divested of their power,
    When youth is robbed of beauty's early flower,
When silver tones like echoes slowly die,
And useless riches all corroded lie—
Thy work shall teach the beauty of His will
When thine own heart is cold and thy lips still;
For unto thee, most honoured among men,
As to another one, He gave—a pen;
His hidden secrets haloed in new light
To thee He whispers, then He bids thee: 'Write!'

The Rose

THEY have consecrated the cathedral!
    I join with those who gaze, praising the architect,
Talking of vision, courage, love and art—
But all the while I'm thinking of the rose,
Her crimson petals, velvet-shadowed heart
Irregular, yet perfectly designed
With poignant and serene simplicity.
On feast days she adorns the new cathedral—
As though Eternity deferred to Time—
Beaming upon our poor, defective gifts
From realms of beauty infinitely pure,
    Whose secret is with God.

Life

A LITTLE candle burning bright
    To show me laughter through the night;
  O kindly flame,
  Life is thy name,
And tender is thy radiant light!

A little candle glimmering low,
A breath may check its fragile glow;
  A brief glad stay,
  And then away,
O winsome flame, I loved thee so!

A little candle dead and cold,
Then o'er the distant hills behold
  The break of day,
  Infinite ray,
Where God has lit a torch of gold.

Crown of Glory

WE strove together for the prize. Today
    His brow is unadorned—or, so they say!
But I see laurels resting there,
More lovely than the crown I wear,
For he has learned to lose with kingly grace,
To triumph though he did not win the race.

Autumn Leaf

A LEAF fell softly to the ground
    First victim of a frosty blast;
Yet, in its autumn face I found
A sign of beauty unsurpassed.

And where the city's dull grey towers
Cast shadows on the dusty street,
I saw the mighty forest, sweet
With scent of cedar, pine and flowers.

So shall a life of purity,
Though borne to earth through wintry chill,
Glow in the darkness, surety
Of perfect purpose, perfect will.

After the death of my brother Sam I visited my sister in Norway whose home is flanked by the vast forest which is their livelihood, and redolent with the scent of cedar and pine. Later an autumn leaf lay on the grey paving stones in front of me remindful of the existence of the forest. As the leaf was a sign of the forest, so a good life lived here and now is all the evidence we need of infinite good beyond our present understanding.

This is the Fellowship

I HAVE a fellowship! Amid the throngs
    I find my friends. I feel their presence, and
Sometimes they touch my hand as, passing by,
They move with silent tread along the years.
No thought is spoken; there's no password; yet
We have a common secret: we are men
With covered fears and sorrows and regrets,
And anguished memories of morns when we,
At the cock's crowing, looked at God and saw
What Peter found in Jesus' eyes—and wept.

Yes, I've a fellowship! It is with men
Whose quiet faces cheer me, for I see
The vision that is calling, calling them
To forge their way through fear, remorse and pain,
And hatred of their weaknesses and sins.
I know; for, in the crowd, I've seen Him, too,
Dressed as a man like us—a Carpenter—
Working and supping with us, speaking, yes,
As though our worthlessness were wealth to Him!
He followed us where no one else could come,
Where'er our footsteps led we found Him there.
And when our shy glance met His certain gaze,
We quivered at the glory shining there,
And our awakened souls cried, ' Thou art God! '

Now? Now we struggle on—for love of Him.
    This is the fellowship!

After the destruction by fire, in 1941, of International Headquarters, the Editorial and Literary Departments were housed in a
rickety old building on Upper Thames Street. Next door, a clean
but rough-and-ready restaurant catered for lorry drivers who,
having travelled through the night, came in for a wartime breakfast.
I preferred this somewhat dingy place to a superior tea-room around
the corner.

Here I met the tough-looking giant who arrived one morning sick and pale, with shaking hands. He had just humanely put to sleep a cat wounded by falling masonry during the night's bombing. A girl, thin and dissipated in appearance, gazed with me at a beautiful crimson rose lone among the ruins of a graveyard adjoining the restaurant. We gazed long and sadly, neither of us speaking until she said huskily: ' Luvly, ain't it ? '

These weary lorry drivers talked quietly about important matters —the long-term effect of evacuation on little children; the fears that made peace-loving men kill each other. I felt at one with them. We shared common perplexities and a deep and terrible yearning for a better world.

I Worship in the Presence of His Faith

HOW did He change the water into wine?
I do not know; I cannot seem to care.
There is a secret—could I make it mine,
I would all other gifts forgo:
How, in such narrow souls, did He divine
Room to receive the truth He died to show?
Room for goodwill to flourish and for love to grow
Till hate should vanish, like the shades of night
Fade when the sunshine spreads upon the morn?
I worship in the presence of His faith in fishermen—
Stupendous trust that saw in minute seeds
Wide, waving harvest fields
Golden in seasons far beyond the day
The Sower's hands were pinioned to a Cross.

I rest in His belief in men like me,
When my soul's deepest well too shallow seems
To hold Love's least intention.

During my student days (and these have never really ended) it was a popular occupation to attempt to rationalize the miracles recorded in the Bible and in so doing overlook the supreme miracle that, by the power of God, could and did take place in men.

These rationalizing attempts seemed like heated arguments about the Latin name of a flower, instead of investigating the hidden life that sent daffodils and crocuses pressing upward through the cobblestones in London. Newly arrived in London from a distant city, the sight of these blossoms amazed and delighted me.

Brief is Our Journey

BRIEF is our journey through the years,
  And fleeting are our longest days;
We cherish every laden hour
  And linger o'er familiar ways;
For toil and grief, or joy and gain,
  When blessed by God, are sanctified,
And friendships forged through serving Him,
  With each new test, are purified.

Yet know we that the sun must set,
  The darkness of the night draws near
When we, as all men, must obey
  The Voice inaudible, but clear,
That calls us from beyond the years,
  Away from all we feel and see;
How shall we bear a last farewell,
  O beauteous world, how part from thee?

With Jesus' name upon their lips,
  The vale of death His servants tread;
In Him they dared believe; in Him
  They dare depart; nor sigh, nor dread;
To Love committing all their loves,
  All counted good through peace or strife,
Content to die believing still
  In Jesus, everlasting life.

47

That devotion to Christ diminishes our appreciation of beauty or lessens our earthly loves has not been my experience. Awakening, often all too slowly, to His glory, we view God's creation with clearer sight whether it be the grandeur of the snow-swathed mountains or the tiny violet hidden in the pine-scented forest. We value our fellow creatures in the light that comes from Him. Thus, though we do not fear death, rarely do we long to depart from our friendly, familiar world. Jesus regarded life as the highest price one could pay to save a friend. Surely, then, the sadness of death can be changed to joy only by Him who is the ' Resurrection and the Life '.

Gay Little Lady

THE gay little lady on our street
   Is old, and her hair is white,
Her form is bent, her step is slow,
   Though her eyes are lustrous bright,
But the soul—the ageless soul of her—
   So straight and strong, so true,
Marches with firmer, surer tread
   Than it could when her years were few.

The gay little lady's eyes can't see
   Me coming down the street,
For the years have stolen away her sight
   And we must guide her feet.
But the soul—the perceiving soul of her—
   Finding His ' staff and rod ',
Sees through the clouds of youth's conceit
   Right up to the face of God.

The gay little lady on our street
Wears faded gowns, and worn,
' Bright colours ', she says, ' are for the maid
    With loveliness to adorn.'
But the soul—the exultant soul of her—
    Is clothed in garments rare,
For she goes out to meet the King
    At the foot of His shining stair.

The gay little lady on our street
    Can't climb the hills today,
Her fragile body is tired and spent
Before we have reached ' half-way '.
But the soul—the tireless soul of her—
    Aspires to a holy plain,
And, leaving me wondering below,
    Scales heights that I'll ne'er attain.

The gay little lady on our street
Will soon—too soon—be gone,
But the beautiful shining soul of her
    Lives on—and on—and on.

Going Away and Coming Back

I'D like to go away
    From the heated walls
Of the city;
From the clanging telephone,
The screeching traffic,
Even the tolling church bells,
Rasping voices and
Blaring instruments.
Oh, yes, I'd like to
Go away, far away—
Where the quiet sun

Announces daybreak when
He caresses his sister
The earth.
Where the stars, silently
Twinkling, take the place of
Glaring street lamps,
And whispering trees or
Murmuring lakes are
Noble substitutes for
Loud voices.
Where the orchestra is
One whose feathered members
Read their music in the skies.
Then, while I'm away—
Far away, I'd like to sit in
The stillness,
And look up into the face
Of Him who loves me,
And whom I love with all
The ability of my
Finite powers.
Then I could forget
All about the noise of earth
With its queer, silly
Grievances that trouble
Some who should not
Be troubled.
I would
Laugh to think that my
Spiritual senses had ever
Been jarred by the clamour
Of men trying to
Speak louder than God.
Feeling the cool touch
Of His hand, I would
Not even remember a detail
Called ' the approval of man ',
Nor would I waste thought

Upon a foolish topic like
' Earthly success '.
In the midst of my tryst
With Him, I would stoop
To kiss the nail-prints
In His hands and feet, or
Reaching upward, caress
The thorn-scars on His brow.
Then quite suddenly
All tiredness would slip
Away, while He told me;
' I suffered much for thee;
What hast thou done for Me ? '
And I would fain
Stay in the silence of
That majestic presence;—but!
I would hasten back to the
Rushing world, the clatter,
And the jeering throng,
To repay Him for the
Nail-prints.
So I am going away—
And coming back!

There was a Seer

THERE was a seer with an eye so keen
    He could discern a joy none else had seen;
The darkened way He walked was bright for Him,
Transparent was the Cross; and o'er the rim
Of death's encirclement He saw the flame
Of God's eternal torches. So He came
To grips with nail and sword and angry men,
His weapon love—and love—and love again.
For love alone could at the last erase
The fearfulness from each unfriendly face.

Beyond, He saw the hand that swung the sword
Binding up wounds; the lips that spoke discord,
In heaven's distances once more He heard
Speaking in union with His Father's word.

Tell me, O Seer, when the teeth of pain
Tore at Thy strength, till quivering with the strain
Thy broken body bade the world believe
What love would bear man's suffering to relieve—
Was it the railing of some drunken foe
That smote Thee sharpest when Thy pulse beat low?
Or the bewildered faces of Thine own, how wise,
Yet watching heaven with sad unlighted eyes?
And was Thy sorrow at the ending lost,
Thy keen eye piercing through to Pentecost?

Only the Men are New

'PRAYER changes things,' they said!
    What things?
  The morning brings
Again some age-old care
For man to take and bear
Over the paths all mortal feet must tread.

I have not known the day
    To change;
    Nor seems it strange,
My friends still carry loads
Up long and lonely roads;
But, I can surely say:

Prayer changes men. 'Tis true!
    And they—
    Looking my way—
Smile 'neath the age-old loads,
Borne o'er the self-same roads,
Only the men are new!

Repose

(O) LOVE, unfathomable, deep,
    Thou who dost waver not, nor sleep,
Encompass me, and I'll not fall,
E'en though I hasten at Thy call:
' Come, O my own, into the night!
Leave the glad fields of joy and light,
Come from the hills and glistening meres,
Into the vale of pain and tears.'
O strong and faithful, earnest Love,
Thy stillness points to stars above,
And 'mid abysmal dark there shines
Treasure once hid in secret mines;
By hill or vale I have no care,
No fear assails—for Thou art there.

Clothed in God

' *If God so clothes the grass. . . how much more will He clothe you,*
    O men of little faith? ' (Luke 12: 28, R.S.V.).

(G)OD clothes the cornflower blue, O blue!
    He gives the lily whiteness, too!
He puts the strength in each slim stem,
And sets the seal of His joy on them!
Out of the earth, the sun, the air,
The flowers drink life from everywhere;
They press above the rain-drenched sod,
The flowers that take their dress from God!

Whisper your secret fragrant flowers!
Can I find God in all my hours?
Reach Him through every circumstance?
And hear Him in the winds of chance?
Can I look up and feel the dew
Of heaven falling on me, too?
Tell me by faith, I soon shall be
Clothèd in God—God clothed in me!

Wings

IF I had wings
    Of faith, the substance of all things unseen,
Then soaring upward I would cease to lean
On faltering clay and paltry mortal show;
Upward toward truth's incandescent glow,
Beyond the tumult, pride and pain of earth,
Within Thy beauteous sphere I'd find new birth;
Like the young eagle I'd go forth, O God,
Till bold and strong I'd mount where Jesus trod
In paths of knowledge of a Kingdom high;
Out of this fragile cell I fain would fly—
    If I had wings.

Alabaster Box

BROKEN the alabaster box;
    The priceless spikenard spilled
O'er ages, and the rarest scent
Poured out upon eternity!
O enemy, who struck the shattering blow,
Now shalt thou never more escape
This fragrance. Everywhere
Like perfumed breezes from the seas of God
'Twill meet thy senses;
Thou must breathe or die!

INDEX OF TITLES

INDEX TO FIRST LINES